Values Education

developing positive attitudes

Tony Eaude

Practical Issues in Primary Education
No 34
National Primary Trust

The Innovation Unit

We work with practitioners, policy makers and others on innovative responses to learning challenges facing the education system. We're a small team of directors who've all had practical experience in schools and LEA's and some of us have also worked in Universities, DfES, GTC and BBC.

What's our aim?

We want to see education professionals working in a system that encourages intelligent and disciplined innovation that genuinely improves teaching, raising standards and makes learning personal and powerful for students. Visit our website to read our latest 'thought pieces' and find out more about our work.

As well as our website you can also discuss the issues raised in this booklet via our online community.
www.standards.dfes.gov.uk/innovation-unit

Schools wishing to know more about Values Education, please contact Neil Hawkes, Senior Adviser, Oxfordshire County Council at neil.hawkes@oxfordshire.gov.uk

Contents

Foreword

Values Education	1
What is meant by values?	2
How children learn about and internalise values	3
The context in which Values Education developed	4
The values on which Values Education is based	5
Transferring Values Education	6
Potential difficulties	7
What this study explored	8
How the research was carried out	9
Case Studies	10
Greenfield Lower School, Bedfordshire	
The Manor Primary School, Didcot, Oxfordshire	
Sussex Road Primary School, Tonbridge, Kent	
Clehonger Primary School, Herefordshire	
The Blake Primary School, Witney, Oxfordshire	
Windmill Primary School, Oxford, Oxfordshire	
Barley Hill Primary School, Thame, Oxfordshire	
Faringdon Junior School, Oxfordshire	
Beenham Primary School, West Berkshire	
The rationale and impact of Values Education	28
Common themes	30
Lessons for other schools	32
Conclusions and wider policy implications	34
Bibliography	36

Foreword

Recently concern about important behavioural questions such as bullying has led to interest in new ideas to deal with the causes. Values Education is among the most innovative. This method of teaching positive concepts to children from the age of five was developed at West Kidlington School, in Oxfordshire. It was so inspiring that I wrote *A Quiet Revolution* about it. Now others are adopting it too: hence this report.

With this method, positive values permeate all school activities, and teachers, parents and children all participate. Concepts such as co-operation and respect form the everyday discourse, so that even young children will ask themselves, 'Should I be doing unity now, or responsibility?' Such clarity is valuable for all children and especially for those whose lives otherwise lack structure.

The schools observed by Tony Eaude had varying motives for introducing Values Education. Some wanted a spiritual lead, some had discipline problems, others needed greater unity. They all made improvements in behaviour, self-perception and relationships. With a shared understanding of common goals, they became more harmonious. Dr Eaude's report provides a clear picture of work in progress and it shows what still needs to be done. The observations indicate that many children showed greater calm, harmony, purposefulness, and capacity for hard work.

One head teacher voiced the views of many: *"Playground squabbles are increasingly rare; children solve their own problems. Our assemblies are thoughtful and reflective. Respect for ourselves and others is more in evidence. When we discussed with Yr 4 children what had changed, they just talked about values! Parents too are very positive."*

I am delighted to commend this report, with its insights into the great possibilities of Values Education.

Frances Farrer
Education journalist and author of A Quiet Revolution

Values Education

Values Education was pioneered at West Kidlington Primary School, near Oxford, following the arrival of Neil Hawkes in 1993 as headteacher. It was developed over several years, attracting considerable interest locally, nationally and internationally. Frances Farrer described what she saw there in A Quiet Revolution (2000), based on many visits during one year. Values Education still continues there but this study examines its adoption elsewhere.

Values Education seeks to address the needs of the whole child, especially personal and emotional development. Though it worked with various emphases, at different levels, the main features were:

- a set of universal values central to how the school works and adults and children conduct themselves and relate to each other;
- explicit consideration, both in assemblies and in specific lessons, of what these values mean, focussing on one each month, based on a cycle of twenty-two values over a two-year period;
- an expectation that all staff model positive values and behaviour to develop a calm and reflective learning environment;
- the use of reflection and visualisation to enable people to control their responses to external events by their internal processes.

As described by Oxfordshire (2002b), Values Education aims to:

> improve the quality of education by promoting a school ethos
> ... underpinned by core values that support the development
> of the whole child as a reflective learner.

This approach was not just individualistic or didactic. Frances Farrer said (in conversation) of West Kidlington, "the children were enabled to perceive themselves simultaneously as individuals and as part of a community". In Neil Hawkes' words, "Values Education is subtle but above all it is about modelling that this is the way we are here. When the teacher does not do it, the children pick this up very quickly."

What is meant by values?

Education has always been about more than the transmission of knowledge. How to develop good and worthwhile qualities in individuals and groups has exercised philosophers and educators ever since the Ancient Greeks thought about what they called virtue, and others character, focussing on personal attributes, such as loyalty or courage. The term 'values' embraces both these and communal or interpersonal qualities, such as unity or respect.

Halstead and Taylor (2000) suggest that values are 'principles and fundamental convictions, ... beliefs, ... ideals, ... and standards'. These guide behaviour and are intimately linked with 'the sort of person one is or becomes' (McLaughlin and Halstead, 1999). It is hard to define what a value is. A loose definition, such as 'a personal quality which a person or group deems of value', offers little guidance as to how values influence behaviour. Tighter definitions tend towards more prescriptive principles or beliefs, regardless of context, requiring less individual judgement. Most individuals, groups and societies wish to pass on their values. Whose responsibility this is may vary. The parent is usually thought to hold the prime responsibility, with aspects supplemented by, or perhaps transferred to, a faith leader, teacher or other respected adults. Outside influences may support or conflict with these influences. The state may have a role through law or regulation, but to what extent is debatable. Education in values is closely intertwined with the aims of education, for an individual or a society.

Values are embedded in all our actions and in the ethos of a school or society, as Jackson et al (1993) explore. Inevitably, children adopt and absorb certain values, both positive and negative, from many sources. Carr and Landon (Halstead and Taylor, 1996) suggest three main processes in moral education: modelling and imitation, training and habituation and enquiry and clarification. One challenge for schools is to help children adopt appropriate values, both implicitly and through explicit reflection on what such abstract ideas mean, so that they understand and internalise them.

How children learn about and internalise values

The development of moral and personal values has traditionally been central to the teacher's role. In Warnock's words, 'teaching is an essentially moral transaction', (Halstead and Taylor, 1996). However, explicit teaching for moral development requires teachers to steer a careful course. In seeking not to indoctrinate children, they may offer too little guidance. Just as too rigid a structure may constrict, an absence of structure may confuse.

McLaughlin and Halstead describe two main traditions of moral education, on a spectrum between what they call non-expansive and expansive approaches. The former emphasises:

- a set of core, or universal, values;
- a specific programme to introduce and re-inforce them;
- a process of values being internalised more by repetition and habit than by conscious reasoning, at least with young children.

An expansive approach highlights that values:

- vary between cultures;
- are internalised more through the hidden curriculum and modelling than direct teaching;
- often conflict, such that children need to learn from a young age how to resolve such conflict by moral reasoning.

These are not mutually exclusive. Any one approach is likely to adopt aspects of each. Both emphasise the inadequacy of an approach that 'anything goes'. In Gutmann's words, cited by McLaughlin and Halstead, 'moral education begins by winning the battle against amoralism and egoism. And ends - if it ends at all - by struggling against uncritical acceptance'. It is not enough merely to teach about values to develop the child's qualities. Children need both to experience what values mean and reflect critically on what is of value. So adults need not just to 'talk the talk, but walk the talk' if children are to internalise values.

The context in which Values Education developed

This booklet describes and evaluates how nine schools adopted an approach called Values Education, as described on p1, to help primary school children up to 11 years old explore and internalise appropriate values. We need to examine the wider social context within which this emerged.

Religion has always been one major source of values. Faith communities may vary in their emphasis on individual or collective values and beliefs, and in the strictness of their expectations, but they offer a tradition of shared values. Warnock (Halstead and Taylor) emphasises that 'the publicity of values, their intrinsically shared nature is of immense importance'. In the last thirty years the influence of organised religion has declined in Western societies. Other, often subtle, influences such as television and advertising have become stronger, encouraging consumerism and individualism. This has coincided with and, arguably, led to greater social instability so that families tend to be diverse in type and less closely knit. The structures supporting positive values are less secure than they were a generation ago. An emerging challenge for schools is both to provide a secure foundation and to help children reflect critically on the values of the wider society.

In the 1990s, there was a sense of concern, at least in Britain, that children were growing up in a moral vacuum. Such terrible incidents as the murders of James Bulger and Stephen Lawrence contributed to this. There was a wider sense that things were not right, and a perception of moral decline and confusion resulting from moral relativism. Documents from the National Curriculum Council, the School Curriculum and Assessment Authority (SCAA, 1996) and Ofsted challenged schools and teachers to address children's spiritual, moral, social, and cultural development. Ironically, this debate coincided with the drive to raise standards of attainment, especially in literacy and numeracy, which may be argued to have emphasised a narrow range of subjects more and these areas less. Values Education was, at least in part, a product of that debate.

The values on which Values Education is based

To what extent it is permissible to instil specific values and what such values should be has been a matter of fierce debate. Values Education draws especially on the non-expansive tradition that there are universal values which, while common to most religious traditions, do not require adherence to a particular set of beliefs. It also draws, especially in its more advanced stages, on traditions of reflection and visualisation within religious traditions.

Neil Hawkes has asked thousands of parents and teachers what qualities they want in their children. He says that twelve almost always appear. These form the basis of a list of twenty-two values, which he argues are universal, constituting a two-year cycle, where one value each month can be displayed, demonstrated and discussed. This has the strength of being an explicit tradition, providing a basis which can be universally (or at least very widely) shared. The twenty-two values are:

Values Directory				
Appreciation	Caring	Co-operation	Courage	Hope
Freedom	Patience	Understanding	Honesty	Love
Respect	Trust	Simplicity	Humility	Peace
Friendship	Tolerance	Responsibility	Quality	Unity
	Happiness	Thoughtfulness		

(Oxfordshire 2002b, opposite p6)

Philosophically, whether these are universal and whether this list is comprehensive is debatable. Some, such as happiness or love, however desirable, seem not to be principles which guide behaviour. Others, such as justice or loyalty, might be included, in addition or as alternatives. In some cultures, values such as modesty or izzat (family honour) might be highly regarded. Whether some values matter more than others is implicit in the notion of core values, sometimes used. How much these claims and objections are valid and matter, in practice, is one question this study explores.

Transferring Values Education

Many of those involved, and visitors, commented on the tremendous impact which West Kidlington made on them, personally, and on the pupils. Something powerful seemed to be at work. The success of Values Education at West Kidlington was, arguably, dependent on some exceptional individuals. Teachers involved directly at West Kidlington, or who had adopted elements in their schools, moved on taking and adapting this approach. In the last five years a growing number of schools in several authorities have explicitly adopted Values Education. The question was 'how well could Values Education be transferred to other schools?'

When Neil Hawkes became Senior Adviser in Oxfordshire in 1999, he developed this work more widely by school visits, speaking at conferences, policy documents such as the Oxfordshire Vision Statement (Oxfordshire, 2002a) and published material such as Hawkes (2003). He, and his colleagues, had been inspired by a range of organisations including UNICEF and the World Spiritual University, and materials such as those of the Human Values Foundation (Auton, 1992), Living Values (Tilman, 2000) and Goleman (1996). Simple summaries were published in Hawkes et al (1997) and Hawkes (2000). Such materials have proved valuable in supporting teachers and spreading the word.

Funding from Oxfordshire County Council and the Innovation Unit at the DfES enabled research into what Values Education looks like in practice in different settings. As an ex-headteacher, and researcher, interested in related areas, but with no direct experience of Values Education, I was asked to:

> 'describe how Values Education has been introduced into nine primary schools, consider the perceived benefits of, and dilemmas implicit in, its introduction and examine the implications for its wider application.'

Potential difficulties

It is often hard to replicate something one admires - or to figure out what makes it work. Here some questions and answers relating to West Kidlington are highlighted.

Is Values Education the answer to all our problems? Neil Hawkes might answer, sincerely but with a smile, 'Yes, ultimately, because it has the potential to deal with the most fundamental aspects of people'. However, Values Education at West Kidlington developed over several years and continues to do so. It was never seen as a short-term, quick-fix solution.

Is it a package or can one take one part only? Values Education is a way of articulating existing features in many good schools. The model can be adapted, but the different strands help to reinforce and enrich each other. The easiest part is investigating the values words, through assemblies and lessons. From this flows an exploration of institutional values and the importance of modelling. The hardest part is the realisation that internal processes help control one's responses to external events, and visualisation which is one tool enabling one to do so.

Is any benefit from Values Education achieved at the expense of standards of academic attainment? It is not possible to be sure of the effect of all the factors which affect levels of attainment. However, the evidence of those who have worked in, and inspected, schools which have introduced Values Education suggest that the calmer learning environment, the clearer focus and the personal qualities developed lead to higher standards.

Is it applicable for all people in all settings? Because the values are seen to be universal and deal with the most fundamental aspects of life, the answer given would be 'Ultimately, yes'; but how it is introduced and developed, and the context, will affect how this is done and how quickly.

What this study explored

This study set out to explore how, and how well, Values Education had worked in nine schools, at different stages of development, and of various sizes and types. Five in Oxfordshire and four elsewhere were chosen and agreed to take part. The research was carried out between November 2003 and January 2004. The intention was to produce an accessible publication for teachers, headteachers and policy-makers, backed by sound research methodology.

It is important to recognise the research dilemmas and limitations. The sample was small and not representative, as all schools were volunteers. As there was limited time this report relies heavily on what was written and said, rather than detailed critical observation. The approach was deliberately unthreatening, but supportively critical, to encourage schools to explore and explain their approach. Broadly common formats for gathering evidence were adopted, but absences and other events meant there were some variations between schools in how the evidence was gathered. Although the aim was to see the schools at work as normally as possible, the observer influence operates especially strongly in such a study.

The key questions to be explored were, in particular:

- why these schools got involved in values education;
- how schools approached its introduction and development;
- what factors helped and hindered its implementation;
- what impact values education has had on the life of the whole school, in particular on ethos, behaviour and academic standards;

and especially considering whether Values Education is appropriate in all contexts, whether the balance achieved at West Kidlington had been achieved elsewhere, and some lessons to learn and pitfalls to avoid.

How the research was carried out

The research involved three main elements to ensure a range of perspectives for the purpose of triangulation:

- a literature search and discussion with Neil Hawkes;
- a questionnaire completed by the nine headteachers;
- a one-day visit to each school.

The questionnaire asked each headteacher to describe:

- the school's distinctive features, such as location, type and size;
- what they understood by Values Education, how long it had been in place, why it was introduced, and next steps planned;
- the roles of those key to its introduction;
- the response of staff, pupils, governors, parents, and any outside bodies, such as Ofsted or the LEA.

The headteachers were also asked for their thoughts and any evidence of how Values Education has affected:

- the school's ethos, curriculum, pedagogy, and academic results;
- pupil attitudes, skills and behaviour;
- staff relationships and morale;
- any other aspect of school life.

They were asked to send the school brochure, and other relevant literature, eg policies and Ofsted or other reports.

On the visits, discussions were held with different groups and individuals. Almost everywhere this included older and younger children, teachers and other staff, parents, governors and the head. Lessons, assemblies, the playground and the school environment, formally and informally, including what was on display were all observed.

Within the project's constraints, the evidence gathered was powerful. This is summarised, with two pages for each school, in the order of the visits, in a broadly common format, before discussing what can (and cannot) be concluded more generally about Values Education.

Greenfield CE (VA) Lower School, Bedfordshire

C of E school in an affluent village. About 120 children, aged 5 to 9. Limited accommodation, much of it temporary, in fairly cramped grounds. Head, Di Thomas, in post since 1997 and recently also head of a nearby school.

In the Head's words, "We'd tried any number of changes to the behaviour policy but it still seemed there was something missing." Hearing Neil Hawkes talk had suggested, 'like a light being switched on', that Values Education might provide this something, a view supported by a visit to a similar-sized school developing it. A visit from him, including a session for parents, had helped convince the governors (who had needed little persuasion) and the wider school community. However, one local resident had spread the idea that it was a criticism of how parents were bringing up their children.

The Head thought imposing a 'values strategy' on schools which did not see the need for it would be disastrous. She highlighted the importance of preparation, especially staff meetings, before Values Education was introduced in 2001. The two-year cycle had been adopted, with a value introduced in an assembly and followed up in other assemblies and class lessons, mostly based on circle time. There is a strong emphasis on public rewards and displays, eg children awarded a leaf to go on a tree in the hall, highlighting what they have done to demonstrate a specific value. Some teachers were developing more use of reflection in class. Even the youngest children were thought to benefit, though observation suggested they found it hard to engage with some values: eg 'safety' had tended to lead to a discussion of keeping safe rather than safety as a value.

Di Thomas had not appointed a values co-ordinator as she felt that this might mean it would not be seen as a whole school issue. There was friendly disagreement on the immediacy of the impact of Values Education, but agreement on it being very much in the process of development. There was a strong belief that a second two-year cycle would lead to some differences of approach, and a cumulative reinforcement of the children's understanding.

Two views were given as to whether, and how, Values Education fits with Church of England status and values, both that it dovetailed well with this, and that it would have been applicable in any case. Di Thomas commented that the differences at the other (community) school where she is Head were the result of a different school context and culture and the personalities involved, rather than this. The Vicar commented how the values cycle provides a structure for collective worship, while expressing some scepticism, though little concern, about whether some were indeed values.

Respect, the first value introduced, was repeatedly cited as the most important. Observation supported the comments of children and adults about improvements in the school ethos, the classroom environment and staff relationships. These seemed to have made a significant, positive difference to staff morale. The impact on parents has been less than hoped for, though many are very enthusiastic. Although it was too soon to judge the impact on academic standards, the improved learning environment, both in relationships and reflectiveness, seemed likely to contribute to children's approach to learning. Ofsted reported favourably on the (less developed) Values Education at the other school where Di Thomas is headteacher. A local adviser who was asked to assess and advise on the work described the process and outcomes very positively.

There was universal agreement that there had been a huge improvement in behaviour. The older children spoke with great thoughtfulness of how the values supported each other. Challenged with, 'if children knew what to say but didn't do it', they agreed this was true of a few, but thought it really had made a difference. In the words of Marcus, aged 9, "Values have helped us in school not only to behave better but also to be more polite to other people."

Summary
Values Education is well established at Greenfield, with a strong emphasis on public recognition of good behaviour. There has been a huge improvement in behaviour, relationships and morale. The older children, especially, are very thoughtful and articulate.

The Manor Primary School, Didcot, Oxfordshire

Community town school, serving an area of socio-economic disadvantage.
About 420 children, aged 5-11.
Head: John Hawkins in post about 6 years, Values Education about 2 years.
Conventional design, spacious grounds.

The Head at Manor, John Hawkins, was enthusiastic and passionate about Values Education. He spoke of how it had helped him 'reclaim the agenda' and said that he was no longer being compromised, because he could bring to his professional life what is most important to him, qualities such as respect and love, in a way that recent developments had made difficult. He said, "It has changed my life". Such language is unfamiliar in the current climate. But, while John Hawkins expressed this passion, he was also a pragmatic man in a demanding leadership role.

The rationale for adopting Values Education was a concern about relationships in the school. In part this had manifested itself in the children's behaviour but the concern was not for 'behaviour as control' so much as enabling individuals to make appropriate choices. So, for example, John Hawkins spoke of how behaviour had improved considerably because inappropriate behaviour was discussed, often in groups, in the context of how it affected others. He stressed the importance of adults living the values consistently.

The cycle of twenty-two values had been adopted. There had been queries about some, such as quality, but staff especially those teaching older children were said not to have found teaching them difficult. The main elements seen were the discussion of values and public recognition of good behaviour in assemblies, how this was used to encourage appropriate and respond to inappropriate behaviour, and enrich PSHE and circle time. For instance, six year olds were given a leaf to put on a 'values tree' to develop their awareness of what the values meant and how they could demonstrate these. Developing more reflection in class time is planned. Notices and displays highlighted values prominently.

While the governors were broadly in support, there had been relatively little discussion of the detail. The parents consulted were supportive of the school but did not know much about what Values Education entailed. Though the Head had provided the main impetus for Values Education, the Deputy (then on maternity leave) had led a group which had given a great deal of thought to incorporating values more explicitly into the vision statement. One priority was to spread the word more widely, for instance by publicising this statement.

The Head argued that Values Education was applicable for all schools, "It has enabled us to establish a rationale for what we are about". He thought that non-Church schools may be able to do such work better, because the whole staff has to work harder, whereas there could be a temptation to 'just rely on the Vicar'. He felt that 'as values goes up the agenda, it affects the decisions you make', thus he had removed the football posts not just because they had led to arguments, but because excluding many children from space for play was in conflict with the school's fundamental values.

The older children especially confirmed that there had been an improvement in behaviour. In a down-to-earth way, they appreciated the explicit messages given while recognising that this influenced some children more than others. They spoke positively about values such as respect, love and friendship, the last of which the younger children also emphasised. John Hawkins said the greatest impact had been on staff relationships and the learning environment: "The value of the month is the easy bit, the demanding end is to get teachers and other staff to take it on board and embody the values. Offering respect is essential if one expects it." A year-on-year rise in academic standards had been sustained, and the Head believed that a positive learning environment had contributed to this.

Summary
The main emphasis is on providing strategies to help children know how to behave, both through awareness of the consequences for other people and explicit rewards. The greatest benefits have been on staff relationships and children's attitudes.

Sussex Road Primary School, Tonbridge, Kent

Community school in a large town.
About 400 children, aged 5-11.
Head: Nigel Amos in post about 8 years.
Original Victorian buildings recently supplemented by extensions.
Grounds adequate rather than spacious.

The Head, Nigel Amos, spoke movingly of reading 'A Quiet Revolution' in late 2001, when he had what he called 'the six-year itch', and being at 'a personal and professional crossroads'. Sensing that the school needed Values Education, he bought each member of staff a copy. They agreed on the need for such an approach and in early 2002 a visit to West Kidlington was arranged. Staff found it hard to articulate exactly what Values Education was intended to address. Among the perceived needs were 'a means of addressing issues surrounding self-image, self-respect and behaviour' and 'a need for calmness, so that life is not so frenetic'.

Several staff meetings were held to decide on the list of values and the detail of their introduction. Initially some adults responded cautiously, with one governor expressing some reservations, but Values Education now seems to have strong support especially among staff. It is seen as providing a clarity and ethos similar to that which Church schools may find easier because of their foundation.

Values Education was introduced in September 2002. Assemblies and lessons build on the value of the month, based on the two-year cycle. The values co-ordinator Nancy Coughlin provides support each month both in writing and more personally being, in the Deputy's words, 'committed to the detail'. Notices and displays ensure that the school's commitment to values and the current value is publicly stated. Systems for recognising positive responses, in work or behaviour, are in place. The approach in lessons varies according to the teacher's confidence, with some discussing values in circle time, others training children in techniques for reflection.

The school has made a big effort to involve parents, as many children were perceived either to be very unfamiliar with discussing such issues or to experience conflicting value systems at home and school.

Those parents consulted supported it very strongly, yet they and the staff recognised that many parents seemed untouched by the school's strong efforts to involve them. Values homework, usually involving discussion of the current value, has met a mixed response. The school has produced and funded for every parent a wonderful calendar based on the values for 2004.

Improved staff relationships and morale were cited as the greatest benefits. Some improvement in children's behaviour was reported, though several challenges remain unresolved. The language of values is often used to deal with inappropriate behaviour and encourage children to reflect on the consequences of their actions. One result is a greater calmness. The classroom environment was said to be more focussed. Although staff were cautious concerning any claim about their role in raising academic standards, several adults were adamant that the calmer learning environment should lead to this! The children spoke more about what happened when they behaved well or badly than more abstractly about what values mean. Most adults and children saw interpersonal values, such as respect, fairness and responsibility, as the most important.

Many people said how much difference Values Education had made, without claiming that it had solved every problem: "Actually changing ourselves to live the values has been the most challenging aspect." The Deputy thought difficult management decisions could test the school's commitment to its values. Helped by an advisory headteacher, a review was undertaken after a year to guide their next steps. The school recognised Values Education as a long but worthwhile process - in the Deputy's words, a 'drip, drip effect which becomes an ocean', but were determined to develop the work.

Summary
Values Education has provided clarity for a positive ethos at Sussex Road. The biggest impact has been on staff relationships and morale, with a calmer learning environment and some improved behaviour. Work with parents is strongly emphasised.

Clehonger CE (VC) Primary School, Herefordshire

C of E village school.
About 130 children, aged 5-11.
Head: Julie Duckworth in post about 1 year.
Children from both relatively affluent and more culturally restricted background.
New buildings and spacious grounds.

Before Julie Duckworth became Head in January 2003, relationships within the school had been difficult and the children's behaviour had been a cause for concern. This had been a major reason for introducing Values Education in March 2003, soon after a recommendation from Bridget Knight, an LEA inspector, who had previously adopted it when a head in Oxfordshire. How the children and staff were seen to relate suggests the view that there had been a rapid change in a short time was justified.

The period of preparation for the introduction of Values Education had been very short. This may be explained by the determination of the Head to get things moving, or the consensus among staff and governors of the benefit of such an approach. The existing aim, based on the acronym CARE, (Challenge, Acceptance, Respect, Excellence) had been revisited in staff meetings. Staff considered how Values Education fitted in with and could contribute to this. There is no values co-ordinator and much of the impetus comes from the Head. No one interviewed made any link between the introduction of Values Education and its status as a Church school.

The two-year cycle had been introduced, with a strong focus on the value of the month in assembly. Respect had been the first value chosen and was seen as one of the most important. The current value, thoughtfulness, featured strongly both in displays and teaching and discussion. The work was followed up in specific values lessons, based on a circle time model. These had been introduced more for the younger than for the older children. The discussions tended to focus on what children should do, rather than encouraging them to reflect on the meaning of the value word.

Governors and parents expressed considerable support for what had happened over the last year. They praised Julie Duckworth's leadership and example. Many children seemed to have adopted the language of values. One parent said how her six year old son 'had told me about co-operation and then, during a dispute about what colour socks he should wear, had said "you're not co-operating".'

One major change was how Values Education had helped to improve the children's behaviour. Both the older and the younger children emphasised the system of rewards, rather than discussing what the values meant, but they thought that things had improved. The Head recounted how two Yr 6 children had referred to the Values work in talking about their dilemma of whether or not to join a group planning to cause trouble in the gardens of local residents.

A second rapid change was in the school's ethos. Improvements in the relationships, both adult-to-adult and adult-to-child, were mentioned frequently. One teacher said that the school was 'more relaxed, open, friendly, less fearful', with criticism more acceptable and less fear of failure. Two support staff separately commented on how this had made the school a happier place. Values Education was still too new to make any secure judgement on the impact on academic standards. The staff certainly believed that its impact on the learning environment would contribute to further raising standards. Ofsted had in May 2003 commended the Head's leadership and the spiritual, moral, social and cultural development.

It is hard to quantify how much these benefits resulted from a new, well-respected head, Values Education or other factors. Arguably, this matters less than how values are lived, which an explicit programme can support and enrich, but never replace.

Summary
There has been a huge change in relationships and children's behaviour in a short time. The explicit structure of values was thought by most concerned to be very important. The impact of a new, energetic Head has been considerable.

The Blake CE (Aided) Primary School, Witney, Oxfordshire

C of E Aided town school, serving nearby villages as well.
About 330 children, aged 5-11.
Acting Head: Marilyn Trigg just started.
Mostly fairly affluent backgrounds.
New and spacious buildings and grounds.

Marilyn Trigg had been in post for less than a term. She previously worked at West Kidlington and is a strong proponent and the main driving force behind the introduction of Values Education. Her approach has been to work closely with the Vicar and the PSHE co-ordinator (who was unfortunately unavailable) rather than involving the whole staff, many of whom have been there for several years.

Although the school provides an orderly and calm learning environment, Marilyn Trigg commented on the children's lack of reflectiveness, highlighted in the 1998 Ofsted report, and their tendency to respond immediately. Encouraging reflection and stillness is a priority. She believes, from prior experience, that Values Education is applicable in all schools but that building on the Church affiliation could provide a good way of introducing aspects of Values Education. For example, the order of the two-year cycle had been based to fit in with the Christian calendar: "The values are complementary to the ethos and (can) deepen it," she said.

The main emphasis had been on introducing a value of the month in assembly. There was a very carefully produced and thought-provoking display on the current value, simplicity. Ideas are also offered to support teachers to follow this up in class, especially in circle time and class-led assemblies. The class teacher with whom I spoke appreciated this and had made some use of it but it was clearly at an early stage.

In discussing the impact, it needs to be borne in mind that Values Education had only been started a few weeks previously. No one claimed that it had made any significant difference to aspects such as behaviour, ethos or academic standards. However, Marilyn Trigg highlighted little things that suggested that children were taking on elements of what she was promoting in assembly.

How the introduction of Values Education had been approached, and comments from staff and parents, suggested that several teachers were yet to be persuaded about it or convinced of its value. This fitted with the comments of parents that the school had always had a strong emphasis on values. They were positive about the previous head's emphasis on 'values as lived', and on the school's Christian values, with the implication that any overt programme is unnecessary. However, Marilyn Trigg had been 'up front' with the governors, when interviewed, about how she intended to introduce this approach and had kept them informed.

While there was less about Values Education to see at Blake than elsewhere, seeing a school at the very start prompts further questions. The children were welcoming, helpful and generally well-behaved and a subsequent Ofsted inspection has praised both this and the PSHE programme in which teaching about values plays a part. However, it was noticeable that the approach of referring to values and involving younger children in discussion was absent. Similarly in the KS2 assembly observed, the children found a time of stillness and quiet reflection, recently introduced, quite difficult as opposed to an expectation which other schools, further along the journey, had managed to foster.

Marilyn Trigg's position was unusual, in that not only was there no obvious problem to be resolved, as at several other schools, but she was both new and had been appointed only for one year. In schools where significant problems were apparent a new approach seemed to make an impact fairly soon. Elsewhere, heads often a few years into post, had taken a long time to prepare the ground and decide which aspects to adopt.

Summary
Values Education was very new at The Blake. Some elements had been introduced, in assemblies, but there had not been a great impact. There was as yet no consensus on the need for an explicit programme. Children were said, and seen, not to reflect explicitly on the consequences of their actions.

> **Windmill Primary School, Oxford**
>
> Community school in Oxford City, serving culturally and socially mixed area.
> About 400 children, aged 5-11.
> Head: Lindsay Weimers, 4 years in post.
> Recent re-organisation has led to major building work and considerable changes.

Windmill was the school with the greatest socio-economic and cultural diversity, with significant numbers from minority ethnic backgrounds. The Deputy, Karen Errington, previously a teacher at West Kidlington, had introduced Values Education as Acting Head. She leads training elsewhere in reflection and visualisation. Its introduction had several rationales: to promote an ethos underpinned by core values, to make assembly more meaningful, to redress an imbalance of frenetic activity and quiet and stillness, and to develop children as reflective learners. There had been unsatisfactory elements of children's attitudes and behaviour, so that there was a 'cycle of fire-fighting' - responding to negative behaviour - and less time 'for each other' and for learning. Values Education was intended to help adults and children relate better to each other.

The two-year cycle had been adapted slightly, for instance omitting simplicity. Displays of the school's aims and expectations were strongly in evidence. There was a clear system of rewards and sanctions, both for work and behaviour. Most teachers taught values lessons, though with different levels of confidence. Karen Errington offers support with ideas, or modelling lessons and reflection and keeping copies of plans. In assembly there was a long, calm period of stillness but several adults commented that encouraging reflection was not easy and it worked better in smaller groups. A group of six year old boys said that they find the reflection time hard. One teacher said, "I'm being honest, reflection is something we could work on. I'm not using it much."

Lindsay Weimers described their approach as 'multi-layered', involving both explicit activities and implicit modelling of the values. Both the Head and Deputy demonstrated a very clear vision, supported by thoughtful policy documents. Building and sustaining teachers' understanding and commitment had not been easy. The question of whether all teachers must always go to assembly had led to a compromise. It seemed that some staff tired, at times, of the regular emphasis on values. However, one teacher informally and enthusiastically described her approach with five year olds, saying that some values were easier to teach, others much harder.

One main benefit was seen to be how teachers saw themselves and related to each other. The relationships and improvements to the learning environment had helped to support hard-pressed staff, though they were still too busy and took too little time for themselves. This was thought to contribute to raised standards, but there was no definitive, hard evidence to support this. Values Education had been one element in improved behaviour, though both adults and children, who emphasised rewards and sanctions a lot, realised that there was more to do. The children were articulate about what values mean and clear about what worked best, seeing stories as one of the best ways of learning about values.

The governors were supportive, with Lindsay Weimers indicating that Values Education has started to influence their thinking. One difficult decision had led to the comment 'that solution wouldn't fit in with our values'. She said that values were regularly mentioned in newsletters and feature prominently in what prospective parents were told. Most had responded very positively, whatever their faith background, supporting her view that Values Education is applicable in every type of school: "values is a helpful idea because it is more inclusive." As one teacher said, "Whatever one's religion, it explores common truths." Another, "There is a common language on how people relate for conflict or praise." Overall, there was an honesty that much had been achieved but that the more difficult, but most worthwhile, aspects of the journey lay ahead.

Summary
Values Education is well established. In challenging circumstances, the benefit has been both subtle and uneven in impact. Relationships among the staff and a structure of expectations have improved. Parents support it strongly.

Barley Primary School, Thame, Oxfordshire

Community school in prosperous town. About 500 children, aged 5-11. Head: John Hulett in post for nine years. Spacious site, modern buildings with extension in progress.

John Hulett had heard of Values Education as the mentor of another head. Barley Hill explicitly became involved about two years ago, with some debate during the first year on which values work best, before starting more overtly with a cycle adapted from the published list. As someone with a distinctive Christian faith and previously head of a Church Aided school, the Head highlighted the dilemmas of collective worship in a community school. He spoke of a 'vacuum to be filled' in post-Christian culture, referring to the lack of 'reference points' for many children. He said how he had been 'running out of hooks on which to hang Christian ideas' and that Values Education provides many good aspects of a Church school without concentrating on one specific faith only. He emphasised that values constantly need to be contextualised if children are to internalise them. He wants to encourage more reflectiveness, since Values Education works at both conscious and subconscious levels.

The Value of the Month is introduced in assembly and followed up both in subsequent assemblies and in classes. This takes place mainly in RE and PSHE, for which the RE co-ordinator provides detailed and regular practical support and resources. Each year group had been given the Values Folder (Oxfordshire 2002b). The school stated its commitment to values quite openly, but with fewer notices or explicit signs and symbols than elsewhere. There is no plan to introduce specific values lessons or techniques for visualisation. John Hulett saw the next step as embedding values in medium term planning, so that Values Education enriches the mainstream curriculum rather than being a bolt-on initiative.

Most teachers' responses (in the Head's words 'a good consensus, though it's overstating it to say that it's enthusiastic') suggested a wish not to overstate the importance of Values Education but to draw useful elements from it. This was reflected in the involvement of governors and parents. Governors support the school's commitment to values through the Curriculum Committee, but it is seen as primarily a curriculum issue. Parents know of it through newsletters, but John Hulett thought it needed to 'go higher profile'.

The children were extremely articulate, with both younger and older children showing that thinking about values is deeply embedded. They frequently made the link between abstract values and specific situations, and saw the values as interlinked, 'all going to make one person'. The older children suggested that too overt an approach could be repetitive and fail to engage many younger children. They thought it needed to be fun, recognising the importance of stories and even suggesting an interactive website!

Children's behaviour had not been a major issue, but the Head thought - and the children's responses especially support this - that the focus on values had made a positive contribution to how children feel about school. Relationships between staff and between staff and children had always been good and the improvements in the school's ethos, both for children and adults, were incremental rather than dramatic. Similarly there had been few concerns about the learning environment or academic standards - though as elsewhere a wish for constant improvement. Values Education is acting more like a reinforcement for what is already good than a necessary agent of immediate change.

Barley Hill had made use of those elements of Values Education offering a structure which is 'positive, neat, memorable and accessible' to make collective worship more meaningful and to enrich existing curricular areas. In that way, it seemed like a quiet rhythm which pulsed through, and provided a rationale for, many aspects to support children's personal and moral development.

Summary
The main emphasis was to support collective worship, RE and PSHE. Values Education has provided a good structure for this, with energetic support. However, it underpins what happens anyway rather than happening in separate lessons.

Faringdon Junior School, Oxfordshire

Community school in a small country town. About 260 children, aged 5-11. Head: Karen Foster, in post about 3 years. Very spacious grounds and buildings currently being extended.

The children's behaviour was a major concern when Karen Foster arrived at Faringdon. She described this in strong language, such as 'mob culture, powerful children, bullying, lack of systems of support for the teacher'. A course led by Neil Hawkes persuaded her that elements of Values Education could help resolve this. "You need something, which needn't be values as such, to identify success other than academic achievement. All are so broad that you can use them and adapt it how you wish," she said. She saw applicability of Values Education to both Church and non-Church schools, and its inclusivity as great strengths.

Values Education has been in place for about eighteen months. The staff had agreed simply to adopt the original two-year cycle, reflecting a pragmatic approach. This is also evident in how they selected only those elements most suitable to their context. However, there was quite a long lead-in time. Staff are encouraged, rather than told, to develop work on values in their classroom practice. Much of this is based in PSHE and RE, especially circle time, with a co-ordinator providing support and resources. The cycle of values, introduced in assemblies and reinforced by notices, displays and reminders underpins this. No specific values lessons or visualisation are planned.

The impact on staff relationships and morale was cited as one major benefit. Several teachers supported this work enthusiastically but without being too earnest. They saw some values, such as humility and simplicity, as 'difficult but good' to teach. On all-encompassing ones, like friendship, 'it's hard not to churn out the usual stuff'. The Head, watching an energetic and ambitious musical practice, commented how such communal activity would have been impossible without the unifying element of Values Education.

The Head argued that everyone, especially children, needs recognition when they do what is appropriate, and that this helps to embed such actions through habituation and feedback. Specific privileges at different levels for Yr 6 children help to encourage good behaviour. The emphasis is on children not being controlled, but learning to be in control, and on child-initiated and child-run approaches. Class discussions reflected this, as did the School Council's involvement in the behaviour policy and the rewards and sanctions used. The maturity and thoughtfulness of the School Council's discussion with me suggests that Values Education can contribute distinctively to the emerging focus on citizenship.

Parents are not involved formally in Values Education but have shown support via a questionnaire. The Chair of Governors (a parent) confirmed that the children's behaviour had been a major concern. Governors were well-informed about and supportive of the approach, describing it as a 'mechanism for dealing with bullying'. She (and others) felt that children being responsible for their own decision-making and supporting each others' had led to much better behaviour and relationships between adults and children. Most thought this improvement in the learning environment must lead to higher standards. Although it is too soon for hard data to support this, Ofsted had reported positively on the effect.

The children indicated how much positive change of behaviour and ethos there had been, saying that it helped most children 'realise what they're doing wrong and how to change it'. They recognised that for a few it was not enough. One boy said, "All the values are important - if you didn't have one of them, the world would fall apart. It's a bit like a wall. The values are like the main bricks and if you took one out, it would fall down." Powerful words!

Summary
Values Education is closely linked with PSHE and consistent, explicit expectations of positive behaviour. Assemblies, circle time and rewards help to reinforce these. There is a strong emphasis on children taking responsibility for themselves and each other.

Beenham Primary School, West Berkshire

Community school serving a mainly but not exclusively affluent area.
About 130 children, aged 5-11.
Head: Sue Butcher, in post about 1 year, previously Assistant Head for 18 months.
New Buildings and spacious grounds.

Values Education was introduced some six months ago, as a result of what were described as disjointed relationships within the staff and with parents. About ten children had been taken to other schools. The emphasis on values was thought to help rearticulate and reinvigorate the school's long-standing ethos and provide a structure for making this explicit for everyone. The Head spoke of how these values do not come naturally to children, in a materialist and egocentric culture. There have been significant changes in teaching staff in the last few years. She thought Values Education had the same effect as (the best aspects of) the religious side of a Church school making it 'easier for everyone to embrace. You need something to pull everyone together - a bond'.

Neil Hawkes had introduced Values Education to the Head when they worked together briefly. After two training sessions he had led and discussion, the two-year cycle of values was introduced, linked to the seasons of the year. Much of the work occurs in assemblies. Sue Butcher modelled and reinforced the relationships and behaviour expected, creating a calm and thoughtful atmosphere, in the assembly observed. Displays of aims and what the values mean and public recognition and rewards are used fairly unobtrusively. Most teachers have started to build values work into PSHE lessons. One teacher introduced 'hope' to her four year olds with great imagination but they found such an abstract notion hard. The Yr 6 children responded quite tentatively, but their teacher saw values work as having transformed their behaviour.

Both the older children and adults, especially the support staff and governors, expressed their strong support for Values Education. The impact on most parents seems, so far, to be limited. The older children highlighted how the work on values had helped to reduce bullying, by making those bullied more able to respond appropriately and bullies more aware of the consequences of their actions. They commented that there was 'more talking things through calmly', and that 'it helps control ourselves a bit more'. One perceptive observation was that, although the direct effect on younger children was less, improving the example which they copied helped indirectly. One less articulate boy, to nods of agreement, spoke of how one young child had 'really calmed down'.

The atmosphere around the school, notably in the dining hall, suggested a strong sense of community. Several adults said that the emphasis on values, and the Head's in modelling relationships especially conflict resolution, had improved the ethos, notably in the relationships between adults. Adults mentioned tolerance, responsibility and respect as the most important values. In Sue Butcher's words, "We seem to keep coming back to them." She highlighted the importance of example and of staff looking both at and after themselves, to encourage and demonstrate the possibility of self-discipline. The children highlighted co-operation, though several thought the values are all interlinked.

It was, as elsewhere, too soon to have hard evidence of any impact on academic standards, but both adults and children spoke of the calmer teaching and learning environment. Both the Head and Assistant Head thought that greater reflectiveness and a calmer lunchtime had improved behaviour and made it easier to teach, and that this was bound to lead to higher standards. Extending the work to all classes and involving parents are seen as the next steps.

Beenham exemplifies how, in some settings, Values Education can provide a spur to significant improvement and highlights the wisdom of a slower, thoughtful introduction to the harder elements.

Summary
Values Education has had a big, immediate impact especially on relationships and behaviour. Modelling behaviour and consistent expectations are seen as central. There seems to be a wish for gradual rather than dramatic development.

The rationale for and impact of Values Education

Before discussing the case studies and the key issues, it is worth reflecting on the visits. All the schools were welcoming, with purposeful and calm learning environments. The enthusiasm for Values Education was very strong. The evidence of two groups was especially powerful. The older children, especially where Values Education had been in place for longer, were both thoughtful and insistent about its importance for them. The two heads who said that Values Education had changed their professional lives and at least four others that it had transformed their schools, all provide strong prima facie evidence of its impact.

However, caution is necessary. The sample of schools was small and self-selecting. Several schools had adopted Values Education relatively recently. The time for observation was short and the approach exploratory rather than critical. Those who spoke out were probably those who were more enthusiastic. Separating the influence of Values Education from other factors would require a much more detailed study - and even then could not be definitive.

Apart from personal experience, two main rationales for introducing Values Education emerge. One was the children's behaviour, the main reason at four schools and part of the reason at three others. However, the need to work at the level of intrinsic motivation, not just rewards and sanctions, was recognised. Unless children's attitudes could be changed so that they became reflective rather than reactive, the reasons for that behaviour would not be addressed. The second rationale related to how to make assembly and collective worship meaningful and to link it with programmes of PSHE and/or RE. At Barley Hill and Windmill this was explicit, but at every school the role of assembly in introducing and reinforcing messages about values was central, with heads, staff and children all emphasising its importance in making it a whole-school issue.

What seems to link these two rationales is the notion of 'something missing'. The clue about what this 'something' was lies in the language used to describe Values Education in practice. Time and again, metaphors of structure, framework and language were used. In the absence of a structure of values, it had become very hard to engage children in discourse or thinking about values. What would previously have come from a faith tradition or from the family was seen, very often, to be absent.

One major strength was seen to be that Values Education is not linked to any one religious group. Those in Church of England schools said that Values Education fitted well with Christian values. Those elsewhere welcomed Values Education as offering a route into discussing the most important aspects of personal development regardless of issues of doctrine, or specific religious beliefs. Few Roman Catholic schools have yet adopted Values Education, maybe because they do not see the need for such a structure.

Repeatedly, relationships between adults were said to be the most important change. Most schools reported an improvement in the children's behaviour, with the children's evidence especially strong. Adults modelling, rather than just talking about, values appeared to have been the most significant factor in influencing children's attitudes. Tellingly, those involved longest were most open about how difficult this is. Superficial change can be rapid; deep-seated cultural changes take far longer. However the explicit structure seemed to have made a big difference for adults and children alike, to many aspects of the school's ethos, above all relationships, and through that the learning environment.

No secure judgement of the impact of Values Education on academic standards emerges from this study. Ofsted, at Greenfield, Faringdon and Clehonger, reported favourably on it. However, most heads, rightly, said it is too soon to tell and obviously many factors are at work. Both heads and other adults kept reiterating how it had improved the learning environment. Their belief was that this enabled more focus and, potentially, more reflectivity. These were important factors in their drive to raise academic standards and enhance children's personal development.

Common themes from Values Education in practice

The case studies show that the schools were at different stages of development and adopted different approaches, depending on their context and priorities. However, common themes can be identified.

On page 1, Neil Hawkes' description of the different levels at which Values Education works is highlighted. Most schools had found adopting the cycle of values easy, with some adaptation and review. It provides a convenient and powerful theme for assembly/collective worship which both adults and children constantly referred to, and related to, children's actions. These were often, but not always, supported by extrinsic rewards. Changing the value each month refreshes and re-focuses both children's and adults' thoughts. This, supported by displays, notices and discussion, provides an effective structure for children to think about what the values mean and how they should conduct themselves. It is a powerful way of making expectation explicit and encouraging children to consider the consequence of their actions and the impact on others.

At several schools, circle times and PSHE lessons especially, were enriched by having a values focus. In specific 'values lessons', practice seemed more varied in type and quality (though the latter is not highlighted in specific case studies and was not the prime purpose of the research). A teacher at Faringdon said how hard it was to avoid facile examples which encouraged compliance rather than exploration of what the value means. This was seen in practice more elsewhere. The problem of contextualising abstract ideas, which the Head at Barley Hill noted, was greater with the younger children. It may be that, as some adults said, it is necessary to reach a second two-year cycle before younger children start to internalise the values. There was stronger evidence of the direct benefit for KS2 children. The older children demonstrated subtle and thoughtful understanding of values. They recognised that for younger children more implicit approaches through example and story might be more appropriate.

How Values Education is conceived, planned and introduced is central to its success or otherwise. This needs time and thought, not only beforehand but in sustaining and enriching the work. The two-year cycle, introduced in assemblies and linked to behaviour and other policies, could have a clear and relatively immediate benefit, as at Beenham and Clehonger. That those schools where Values Education was most embedded were those which struggled most with the next steps suggests that the harder levels need to be developed slowly, thoughtfully and organically. Continued work to build staff understanding and classroom expertise seems a longer-term and more difficult task, both to develop pedagogical approaches and to help with sustained reflection or visualisation, of which the only evidence seen was at Windmill and Sussex Road.

There were different views about having a Values co-ordinator. Where there was one, their enthusiasm, resourcing and prompting was greatly valued. Elsewhere the idea had not been adopted. This may be related to school size, as the direct influence of the head possible in small schools may be diluted in larger ones. However, at Greenfield the Head was concerned that such an appointment might marginalise Values Education into 'another subject'. The importance of the head's role in leading development in values was highlighted in a survey by Taylor (Halstead and Taylor, 2000). This has been implicit in this study, but evidence from adults and children at every school was that such leadership was necessary, though not sufficient, to guarantee success.

Schools had adopted those aspects of Values Education most suited to their own context and concerns. The process of review and discussion at Sussex Road and Windmill, the 'constant tweaking' mentioned by the Head at Beenham and the whole approach at Barley Hill, Faringdon and Greenfield all reflect the importance of pragmatic responses rather than an inflexible template. The subtlety of working with fundamental attitudes is reflected in that no school demonstrated any one aspect not found in many schools elsewhere. What was remarkable was how several elements, each on their own unremarkable, combined to make a significant impact. Systematic engagement with these ideas harmonises the staff and provides security and focus for the children.

Lessons for other schools

The rationale for introducing Values Education varied, though with common elements. But the rationale must emerge from an evaluation of the school's needs, not be imposed. The pressures on schools and teachers are intense. Any new initiative seen as 'extra' may be unwelcome in many schools. External advice and evidence that it is manageable was important in almost all schools. To work effectively staff must believe that Values Education is manageable and achievable. This is not to say it is necessary to have everyone on board from the start. Of course the level of enthusiasm was variable though enthusiasm seemed to grow rapidly, especially when there was a recognition that different adults could work at their own pace within a supportive framework.

The schools flexibly adapted the programme to their own contexts. Words do not fully capture the inventiveness of ideas such as the calendar at Sussex Road, the values tree at Greenfield and the resource banks at three schools, but they were deeply impressive.

The effect on staff relationships and morale was frequently cited as the most positive change, including support staff as well as teachers. For example, the office administrator at Clehonger had responded positively. This should encourage those who are uncertain of the benefit of Values Education. Several schools recognised how important it is for all staff to 'walk the talk' but how tricky it is to ensure consistency from all staff, including lunchtime supervisors.

While the wish to involve governors and parents is understandable, especially if the long-term aim is a change of culture, this study suggests that initially the full involvement of governors was desirable rather than essential. Given the evidence of Sussex Road, Manor and Windmill, the active involvement of parents is a long haul, especially in more challenging contexts. Both an explicit approach, as with Windmill's induction and Sussex Road's homework, and a quieter one, influencing parents through the children, may be appropriate.

The benefits of Values Education leap out from the case studies. The impact on behaviour and relationships was often articulated. The children, especially in KS2, had an impressive ability to reflect on the values. Children's involvement, as in School Councils or setting up rewards systems, seemed to enhance this and it seemed to grow with time. Any suggestion that children forget one value once a new one was introduced was dispelled by how they connect the values, as in the metaphor of the wall at Faringdon. The changeover each month seemed to provide fresh impetus.

Most adults and children saw the communal and interpersonal values, especially respect and co-operation, as the most important. This seems to reflect the wider social worry about individualism and the weakening of family and Church structures. Values discussions in assemblies and in class often emphasised individual achievement in the context of collective goals. The way in which helping individuals was seen as a whole-class responsibility at Faringdon or the collective strategies to support children's behaviour at Manor can help dispel worries that Values Education may be too individualistic.

Whether or not the values are universal, whether those cited on page 5 should be adopted and whether such issues matter is a question for debate. The evidence was strong that most adults were not too worried, as long as the list remained flexible. The Vicar at Greenfield thought that some are not values, but that this did not detract from the importance of discussing values. However, it may be that the difficulties highlighted with the youngest children could be reduced either by a revised list, or by the use of stories, drama and play, to help children understand them more substantially.

The need for care and training in introducing values lessons has been highlighted. A more basic curricular issue was whether the reflective emphasis of Values Education might conflict with other prevailing messages about the importance of pace in teaching. There was evidence that this tension existed. This is beyond the scope of this study but it may be that Values Education has an important role to play in enabling children to develop their reflective abilities. This could be one element of its contribution to academic achievement as well as personal development.

Conclusions and wider policy implications

This study suggests that Values Education has great potential to provide a structure and framework to help staff and children develop a language and a way of discussing and understanding difficult, often unfamiliar, aspects of moral education. Apart from The Blake, where Values Education was in its infancy, the greatest impact was in relation to staff relationships and morale and children's behaviour and attitudes. The benefit seemed greatest for those children whose behaviour had been reactive and lacking in adult direction. Unsurprisingly, the effect on the most challenging children was much slower. The long-term effect on standards is less clear but most heads and teachers believed it would be positive.

The rationales given for introducing Values Education testify to the need for a structure for approaching moral education. The enthusiasm of most involved for its benefits was extremely striking. Part of its power seems to be its combination of structure and adaptability in drawing on features of many religious traditions.

Values Education requires the active commitment of the head and most if not all the staff: "If you're not fired up, then the children won't be," one teacher said. Everywhere, the importance of all adults modelling good behaviour and the values underlying it was re-iterated. If values are only spoken about and not demonstrated, it is unlikely to have a positive impact and may be counter-productive.

Values Education must not be seen as a short-term solution. While in schools such as Clehonger and Beenham improvements had occurred rapidly, this could be put down to a new and energetic head introducing changes where, for different reasons, these were needed. But the experience of West Kidlington and those, such as Windmill and Sussex Road, involved for longest was that the harder elements of Values Education took a long time and were, indeed, hard to achieve. However, with a thought-out rationale and sensitive leadership, potentially it seems to be applicable in all schools, Church or community, urban or rural, large or small.

The impact of Neil Hawkes, and the example of West Kidlington, both through 'A Quiet Revolution' and visits, was considerable. Every school emphasised the importance of hearing or seeing how Values Education worked in practice, by visits, talks or training sessions. Resource materials and books can support such work but are no substitute for personal experience.

How Values Education was introduced was crucial; how it was sustained even more so. In the words of the Head at Manor, "It's an initiative which lends itself to a gentle evolution." Remarkably few difficulties in introducing it were evident, though these included the possibility of misunderstanding or wariness of what it was about (as at Greenfield, Sussex Road and Windmill), a belief that an explicit programme is not necessary, and introducing the more challenging elements too rapidly. Values Education is not something to be imposed but to be offered and supported where appropriate and enabled to grow organically.

This has important implications for dissemination. In the words of the head at Greenfield, "The last thing we need is a values strategy." Values Education could be allowed to spread slowly, by word of mouth and training at local level, but this would limit its potential. If there is to be national dissemination, locally delivered training and support groups will be essential. The chance for schools to develop this work so that others can experience it in action - maybe on a Beacon school model - is worth considering. Video material may also be effective. Without such opportunities the central messages of Values Education may too easily be diluted.

Extravagant claims from such a small-scale study are inappropriate, but the evidence suggests that important and positive lessons can be learnt. However, more detailed, longitudinal, research will be required to confirm these findings. With these provisos, Values Education clearly made a tremendous impact in a range of schools, from experienced heads to young teachers, from streetwise ten year olds to five year olds just starting in school. Maybe the last word should rest with Philip, a ten year old at Greenfield. He said with great feeling, and backed by nods from other children, "I was always in trouble but now I never am."

Bibliography

Alderman C, (1995) *Sathya Sai Education in Human Values,* Pinner: Sathya Sai Education in Human Values of the UK

Auton J, (1992) *Education in Human Values* (www.ehv.org Human Values Foundation)

Farrer F, (2000) *A Quiet Revolution*, London: Rider

Goleman D, (1996) *Emotional Intelligence*, New York: Bantam

Halstead JM, and Taylor MJ, (eds) (1996) *Values in Education and Education in Values*, London: Falmer

Halstead JM, and Taylor MJ, (2000) *The Development of Values, Attitudes and Personal Qualities: A Review of Recent Research*, Slough: National Foundation for Educational Research

Hawkes N, Keeping I, and Heppenstall L, (1997) *Values Education*, Primary Practice No 10, 14-18

Hawkes N, (2000) *Being a School of Excellence,* Primary Practice No 26, 10-17

Hawkes N, (2003) *How to Inspire and Develop Positive Values in your Classroom*, Wisbech: LDA

Jackson PW, Boostrom RE, and Hansen DT, (1993) *The Moral Life of Schools*, San Francisco: Jossey Bass

Lickona T, (1991) *Educating for Character: How Our Schools Can Teach Respect and Responsibility*, New York: Bantam

Oxfordshire County Council, (2002a) *Education in Oxfordshire, A Vision for the Future*, Oxford: Oxfordshire County Council

Oxfordshire County Council, (2002b) *Values Education: Resource Pack for the Primary School*, Oxford: Oxfordshire County Council

McLaughlin TH, and Halstead JM, (1999) 'Education in character and virtue' in Halstead JM, and McLaughlin TH, (eds) *Education in Morality*, London: Routledge, pp132-163

SCAA, (School Curriculum and Assessment Authority) (1996) *Education for Adult Life: the Spiritual and Moral Development of Young People*, London: SCAA

Tillman D, (2000) *Living Values: an Educational Program*, Deerfield Beach: Health Communications Inc